MVFOL

BL: 3.7

AR Pts: 0.5

Saltypie

A Choctaw Journey
from Darkness into Light

by TIM TINGLE

Illustrated by

KAREN CLARKSON

A bee sting on the bottom! Who could ever forget a bee sting on the bottom? Not me. I felt the sting, slapped my pants, and ran to a wooden bench in the grape arbor.

I sat there crying till Mawmaw, my grandmother, came and sat beside me. "Didn't you hear the bees?" she asked.

"No," I said, wiping my eyes. We sat still as dawn. After a moment I could hear the bees, buzzing and humming in Mawmaw's white gardenias.

"That was some kind of saltypie, that bee sting," Mawmaw said. She smiled her sweet smile and laughed her sweet laugh till everything hurtful went away.

A soft breeze blew in. Mawmaw stood up and in that shuffling way she had of walking, she moved towards the chicken house, calling over her shoulder, "Chickens need feeding."

"Chick-chick-CHICKENS!" Mawmaw called out. Hundreds of chickens came running and we tossed the feed into the air.

We filled a tin bucket with eggs and carried them to a small room in the back of the garage, where my Pawpaw had built a light board. He had replaced a porcelain tabletop with glass and wired four light bulbs under it. When Mawmaw flipped the switch, shafts of yellow light rose to the ceiling.

Mawmaw placed the eggs on the table. I rolled them over and over, looking closely for blood spots on the yellow yolks. "There's one, Mawmaw!" I shouted. I handed the egg to my grandmother. She held it close to her eyes.

"You're a good boy," she said, laughing her quiet funny laugh, like there was so much more to laugh at than you would ever know. "That's some kind of saltypie for those chicken eggs, boy," she said, tossing the bad eggs in the trash bucket.

My grandmother was a strong and special Choctaw woman. Everyone who knew her knew that. In 1915, when my father was almost two years old, the family left Oklahoma. They moved to Pasadena, Texas, to a white wooden house on Strawberry Lane. The first morning in her new home, my grandmother stepped quietly on the front porch to greet the dawn.

She never saw the boy who threw the stone that cut her face. It sent her stumbling inside the house, slamming the door behind her. She slid against the surface of the pine door and crumpled in a heap on the floor, sobbing.

My father was two at the time. He ran to see his mother sitting on the floor, her hands covering her face. It looked like the peep-eye game to him.

He crawled into her lap and saw shiny red liquid squishing from between her fingertips. It reminded him of sweet cherry pie filling, bubbling up from the criss-cross crust of Mawmaw's pies. He reached to her face to get a taste of it, then touched his fingertip to his lips.

"Saltypie!" he said, spitting as he said it. "Saltypie!"

Mawmaw pulled her hands apart
and held her little boy close.

   "Saltypie," she said, nodding her head.
"That sure was some kind of saltypie."
Then she started laughing, laughing and
crying, rocking back and forth and saying,
"Sure enough, that was some kind of saltypie
with those rocks. Some kind of saltypie, boy."

At the supper table that night, Mawmaw laughed when she told Pawpaw what had happened.

"You should have seen our little boy," she said. "Saltypie! That's what he said. Saltypie!"

"I'll find out who did this!" Pawpaw said, rising from the table.

Mawmaw grabbed his arm and said, "Your going won't do any good. I never saw the boy who threw the stone."

In 1954, when I was six years old, Mawmaw and Pawpaw still lived in that same house, the house of yellowjacket bees! One morning Pawpaw told me I could have my own cup of coffee for breakfast. I sat next to him while Mawmaw circled the table, filling up the cups.

Mawmaw put her thumb in my Pawpaw's empty cup and poured the coffee. Then she shook the hot coffee from her thumb, licked her thumb and put it in the next cup. When she came to me, I put my hand over my cup. I didn't want her thumb in my cup!

Everybody stopped talking. A chair scraped. I looked up and saw my Aunt Bobbie coming for me. I sat frozen in fear.

Aunt Bobbie scooped me from the chair and carried
me to the back porch. I expected a whipping. She
gripped my arm and I made a scrunching face.

Nothing happened. I opened my eyes.

"You don't know, do you?" she said.

I shook my head.

"Bless your heart," she said. "You don't
know. Your grandmother is blind. That's
why she puts her thumb in the coffee cup,
so she'll know when the cup is full."

I couldn't believe it. I was six years
old and I didn't know my grandmother
was blind. Aunt Bobbie smiled.

"Just go back in there and let your
grandmother do what she has to do."

That night at the
evening talking time, I
asked my Uncle Kenneth,
"Why is Mawmaw blind?"

"Her eyes went bad.
Something she was born with
caught up with her," he said. "You
know, your Mawmaw has had a hard
life. But she's happy now. She's a strong
woman, stronger than that boy with the
stone, don't you think?"

"You bet!" I said. "But who threw the stone?"

"I don't reckon we'll ever know who did
that," Uncle Kenneth said. "That was
some kind of saltypie, that stone and
your Mawmaw."

He sat without talking for a long time.
We listened to the sounds of the chickens
roosting. At Mawmaw's, it always seemed that
if you waited quietly, you could know things that
ought to be known, hidden in the sounds.

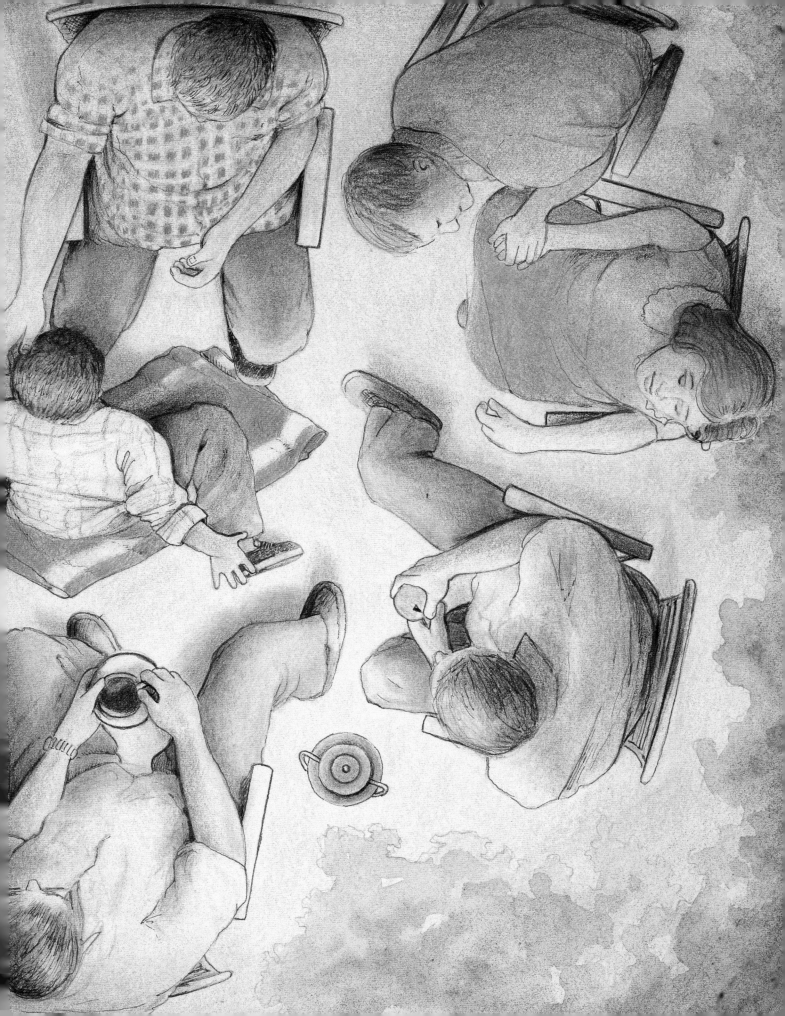

"Why did they throw the stone?"

"Your grandmother was Indian. That was enough back then," my uncle said. A mosquito buzzed around my ear. I started to slap it, but a little breeze blew up, carrying the mosquito off and washing the backyard with the soft music of rustling corn stalks.

"What is saltypie?" I asked him.

"It's a way of dealing with trouble, son. Sometimes you don't know where the trouble comes from. You just kinda shrug it off, say *saltypie*. It helps you carry on." I fell asleep that night to the sweet aroma of gardenias, blooming white and tucked real close to the house.

The years passed by taking forever.
In 1970, I was a junior in college. I was
studying for an exam when the phone rang.
   "Your grandmother is in the hospital!"
Aunt Bobbie said. "Come right away!"
   I drove four hours to the hospital and dashed
inside. The waiting room was filled with
people, sitting and standing everywhere. The
whole Tingle clan was gathered together! My
father stood to greet me.

"Your grandmother is having an eye transplant," he told me. "We may be waiting for days before the doctors know anything."

We did wait for days, catching up on news and laughing at old stories, as families do. About an hour before sundown of the fourth day, the doctor stepped among us. "We'll know soon," he said.

A quiet but remarkable change occurred in the room. The light streaming through the window took on a copper glow, floating above the green waiting room carpet. It reminded me of the late afternoon sun in Mawmaw's backyard.

The spirit of who we were as a Choctaw family was coming alive in the room. We could almost hear the cicadas hum their night music in the Choctaw river bottoms of years ago. The stories continued, but there were fewer words now and much silent nodding. Many heads were bowed to the moment.

My Uncle Boyd told about how
hard it had been for Mawmaw
as a little girl at Indian boarding
school, Tuskahoma Academy in
Oklahoma, especially after her
father died and there was nobody
to take her home for Christmas.

We listened like we were all sharing the same sweet dream for over an hour, till everybody had spoken except my father. He stood up and took his cap off, twisting it in front of him.

He was shy and kept us waiting for a long time. The doctor peered through the door and motioned to him. They spoke in the hallway and my father returned.

It was so right that my father, who had given us this word fifty years ago in a moment of childhood mis-understanding, would now take it away in a moment of enlightenment. He lifted his eyes and spoke.

"No more saltypie," he said. "Mawmaw can see."

It seemed like all of Mawmaw's troubles, and all of our Choctaw troubles, had led up to this moment.

"No more saltypie. Your grandmother can see."

The next morning Aunt Bobbie lined up all thirty-two of the grandchildren, myself and my cousins, outside of Mawmaw's hospital room.

"Your grandmother wants to guess who each of you are," she said. That's when I realized Mawmaw had never seen any of her grandchildren. Aunt Bobbie hugged us one at a time and whispered, "When you enter the room, be sure to tiptoe. If you walk in your usual walk, she will know who you are by the sound of your footfall."

That is the real blessing of my grandmother. Blind as she was, she taught so many how to see.

We all leave footfalls, everywhere we go. We change the people we meet. If we learn to listen to the quiet and secret music, as my Mawmaw did, we will leave happy footfalls behind us in our going.

How Much Can We Tell Them?

MY FATHER was the finest welder I ever knew. He welded together pipelines that carried oil beneath the ground. He could make anything out of iron—a swing set for a playground, a flagpole, a bicycle rack, even a ring with my brother's initials. My father was an American Indian, a member of the Choctaw Nation of Oklahoma.

My grandmother, my father's mother, grew acres of vegetables and raised chickens, both for the meat and for the eggs. She was also an Oklahoma Choctaw. As a child she attended an Indian boarding school, where she was punished for speaking her language, the Choctaw language. She was determined that all of her children graduate from high school, which they did.

My Aunt Juanita was Choctaw, too, an American Indian like my dad. She married a dairyman with a hundred cattle. They lived in Cypress Fairbanks, west of Houston.

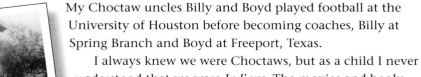

My Choctaw uncles Billy and Boyd played football at the University of Houston before becoming coaches, Billy at Spring Branch and Boyd at Freeport, Texas.

I always knew we were Choctaws, but as a child I never understood that we were *Indians*. The movies and books about Indians showed Indians on horseback. My family drove cars and pickup trucks. Movie Indians lived in teepees. We lived in modern houses. Indians in books and on television hunted with bows and arrows. My father and my uncles hunted, too, with shotguns, but mostly they fished. They kept my grandmother's freezer filled with fish from Galveston Bay.

Were we real Indians? Yes. We still are real Indians, modern Indians. Like many Americans, we celebrate our history, our Choctaw-American history. We know our history never included teepees or buffaloes. We were people of the woods and swamps of what is now called Mississippi. Early Choctaws had gardens and farms. For hundreds of years, they lived in wooden houses. Education of the young was always important. Young men served in the Choctaw military, not as braves or warriors, but as highly respected defenders of our homes and towns.

Long before explorers arrived from Europe, we had a government, a Choctaw national government. We selected local and national leaders. We recognized women as equal citizens. In truth, women were the principal landowners, so it could be said that *women recognized men as equal citizens*. My grandmother's natural guidance of the Tingle family is a continuation of this tradition, with women as leaders.

In 1830, the Choctaw Nation was forced to move west in a great American tragedy, the Trail of Tears. In many ways the story *Saltypie* is a continuation of this trauma of removal. When my grandmother felt the sting of a stone thrown by a young man who knew nothing about her, only that she was Indian, the fears returned. People respond to trauma in many ways, but a very natural response is to cling to family.

As a book of family bonding, *Saltypie* will touch the hearts of readers. Passing references to the Indian boarding school experience and the Trail of Tears will sound familiar to many. But there is a nagging problem in *Saltypie*: the boy throwing the stone. Who is *he* and why is he doing that?

I feel that I should motion to you now, quietly and in tiny gestures unseen by anyone else, so I can share a whispered secret, a secret only a few outside of Indian Country even suspect. Are you ready? Ok. *Listen closely.* Indians know of many wrongs done to them and their friends and relatives that we seldom speak about. When Indian storytellers and writers get together, we often ask, "How much can we tell them?"

How much can we tell them before they cover their ears and refuse to listen to our stories? Many non-Indian people have difficulty believing that bigotry could still be alive, or could ever have been alive, in the settling of our nation, in our dealings with Indians.

Who is that boy and why did he throw that stone?

Consider the following stereotypes: While some Indians were savages, most Indians were gentle lovers of nature. Indians dressed in beautiful beaded animal skins and eagle feathers. Most Indians followed the buffalo, ate the buffalo, and lived in teepees made from the buffalo. Indians were brave but unable to survive in the modern world. We saved the Indian. We educated the Indian.

Most children's literature available in libraries today promotes these stereotypes. Make no mistake; these *are* stereotypes.

"How much can we tell them?"

Can we tell them that the vast majority of children's books written about Indians in America were not written by Indians? Can we somehow convince them that this matters?

I know. To many readers this thought is new.

Here is an idea, a simple one. To teachers and parents who want to help displace the stereotypes about American Indian people, at some point during the reading of *Saltypie*, ask your listeners, "What do Indians wear?"

Smile and nod at the answers. *Moccasins, feathers, beads, animal skins.* Then tell your students and children, in your own words, "If I were you, I would have probably said the same thing. But your answers are not correct." Then hold the

book up for students to see, any page will do.

"This is what Indians wear. Indians are modern people." Enjoy the sound of your voice saying these words. The sound of spoken truth is beautiful and strong.

If the dialogue about American Indians is to have any true importance, it must begin with this understanding: Indians are modern people. Indians serve in the United States military, as soldiers, sailors, and marines. Indians are schoolteachers, lawyers, businessmen and women, home builders, doctors, and writers.

So, who is that boy and why did he throw the stone?

Maybe it was a stone of misunderstanding, thrown by a boy who simply didn't know. He didn't know that Indians are Americans, that Indians are modern people, that Indians are friendly neighbors who love their families, their homes, and care about education. If we can assume he didn't know, let us forgive him. Let us teach his grandchildren, so they will pocket their stones and extend a hand in friendship.

In 1963 President John F. Kennedy said, "For a subject worked and reworked so often in novels, motion pictures, and television, American Indians are the least understood and the most misunderstood of us all."

Might we now begin—one parent, one child, one teacher, one classroom at a time—a real and more truthful education about American Indians.

We are a nation dedicated to the freedoms so aptly voiced in the Bill of Rights. Freedom is for all Americans, for all colors and blends, for all beliefs. We, as a people, celebrate the revealing of previously hidden truths. If wrong exists, we want to know it. We want to change it. If wrongs existed in the history of our nation, we want to hear of them. And why? My Choctaw friend Tony Byars, an Indian boarding school attendee and celebrated United States Marine, said it best. "We want to know of these wrongs," said Tony, "so they will never happen again."

Now is a great time to be an American Indian.

To my sister Jeanne, the most beautiful of all Choctaw fire-baton twirlers. —Tim Tingle

To my daughters, who taught me what it is to love. —Karen Clarkson

Visit us at www.cincopuntos.com or call 1-915-838-1625.

Cinco Puntos Press

Book and cover design by Vicki Trego Hill of El Paso, Texas. Printed in Hong Kong by Morris Press.

Saltypie: A Choctaw Journey from Darkness into Light. Copyright © 2010 by Tim Tingle Illustrations copyright © 2010 by Karen Clarkson. All rights reserved. No part of this book may be used or reproduced in any manner whatsoever without written permission except in case of brief quotations for reviews. For information, write Cinco Puntos Press, 701 Texas, El Paso, TX 79901 or call at (915) 838-1625. Printed in Hong Kong. FIRST EDITION 10 9 8 7 6 5 4 3 2 1

Library of Congress Cataloging-in-Publication Data. Tingle, Tim. Saltypie : a Choctaw journey from darkness into light / by Tim Tingle ; with illustrations by Karen Clarkson. — 1st ed.   p. cm.   ISBN 978-1-933693-67-5 (alk. paper) 1. Tingle, Tim—Childhood and youth—Juvenile literature. 2. Tingle, Tim—Family—Juvenile literature. 3. Choctaw Indians—Biography—Juvenile literature. 4. Grandmothers—United States—Biography—Juvenile literature. 5. Wisdom—Juvenile literature. 6. Choctaw Indians—Crimes against—Texas—Pasadena—Juvenile literature. 7. Blindness—Texas—Pasadena—Juvenile literature. 8. Pasadena (Tex.)—Biography—Juvenile literature. I. Clarkson, Karen. II. Title.   E99.C8T55 2010   973.04'97—dc22 [B]   2009042859